MIND YOUR BEESWAX

By Zagros Bigvand
Illustrated by Aaron Onsurez

Dedicated to
the people that have touched my life
and have shown me that they can succeed
by helping others succeed.

Dedicated to my Mom,
Mastaneh Bigvand
I Love You.

ACKNOWLEDGEMENTS

In a book on generosity, it is only fitting that I acknowledge some public figures as well as individuals who have impacted me in my life. American society provides several public examples of influential generosity. Bill and Melinda Gates, entrepreneurs, philanthropists, and founders of Bill and Melinda Gates Foundation, and Warren Buffet, extraordinary business man and philanthropist, model the idea that individuals should do more than just make money with their lives. They remain examples of charity, innovation, and hope. They made their money and are spending the rest of their lives helping the world with their fortunes.

Oprah Winfrey is my hero. She tops my list of publicly generous individuals. She came from nothing and has built an empire by sharing her life with people and by bringing socially conscious topics to the forefront of public discussion. She has used her life and wealth to provide a stage for confronting important issues and helping others live more successful lives.

In my own life, I need to recognize two formative, professional influences. The first is Professor Jay Hammond, a history professor at Brookhaven College in Dallas, TX. It was in his class that I first learned to think outside the box and to question everything. He always asked, "Why?" I learned from Professor Hammond to do the same. Second, I need to thank Kevin Miller, founder of TexasLending.com. I encountered Kevin about a year after my start-up software company went under. I was down both financially and mentally when I went to work at TexasLending.com. He placed a desk for me in his personal office and he showed me everything I needed to know about the mortgage banking business. An example of the countless nuggets of wisdom I've learned involved watching sports. One day I wanted to leave the office to watch a Mavericks game at a sports bar. Kevin said, "Watch them play but what you are really doing is watching them make money. When is the last time they came into this office and watched you make money?" He was right. I stayed in the office and called clients instead. I don't watch sports much anymore. I was 24 years old when I started working for his company and by the time I was 28, I was a millionaire.

For this book, I want to thank Jeff Crilley my dear friend who I'll always be grateful to for inspiring me to write this book. He and I were sitting at a Starbucks discussing different publicity ideas for my real estate brokerage. I mentioned in passing that I wanted to write a book but was uncertain about the project. He is the one who pushed me to write a book and tell my story. I also need to thank my friend Herro Mustafa who gave me the inspiration to intertwine social and environmental consciousness into my businesses. Ultimately this led to the idea for Mind Your Beeswax. Herro introduced me to two dear friends, Kirk Roos and Janet Klein. These two generously gave their time to this project by being a sounding board and helping me work out my ideas. I must have called them a thousand times each getting ideas about this project. I need to thank my dear friend D'Andra Simmons for inspiring me to donate all proceeds of the sale of this book to charitable causes. I've never met anyone with more philanthropic leadership then D'Andra.

My family is my life. They are the oxygen in my lungs and the blood in my veins. My sister is my best friend. My father showed me that taking calculated risks in life is the only way to make it. My mother has been my inspiration, champion, and greatest influence of all.

Thank you all for making such an impact in my life. I respect and dearly love all of you and hope that I can do for others what you have done for me.

CONTENTS

CHAPTER ONE

The buzzing in the hall was deafening. As the queens and their aides stared at the screens, cries of disbelief echoed around the chamber. Then all at once, silence, as if someone had punched the "mute" button. The members of the B-8 summit digested the troubling statistics that had generated this emergency meeting:

- Tropical Hives: 30% dead

- Desert Hives: 35% dead

- Subtropical Hives: 25% dead

- Eastern Hives: 40% dead

- Island Hives: 30% dead

- Western Hives: awaiting data

- In the last week alone, 50 hive deaths have been reported.

As the current B-8 Chair-Bee, Nectarina, took the podium, a flurry of wings from the adjoining chamber announced the arrival of a U.H. emissary. She zoomed to the front of the room, whispered something to the Chair-Bee, then flew away. Nectarina looked grave.

"My fellow Queens," she began, "Though these statistics are sufficient to provoke concern, I have just been given news that elevates the situation to one of pandemic. The first Western Hive has fallen! Not only have 32.8% of world hives now imploded, but the crisis has reached Developed shores!

"Our analysts are working overtime to understand the causes of this catastrophe, but as yet we have no answers. In part, this is because we arrive on the scene after the disaster has occurred and find only an empty hive with little to indicate the fate of its inhabitants. In conjunction with remaining local hives, we have formed forensic teams, which are working around the clock to gather data. We hope to have answers soon. In the meantime, I have called this meeting to see if our collective insights can provide solutions," ended Nectarina.

She had hardly finished speaking when Beelzibar, Queen of Hive Chernoboch, ferociously responded. "I am sure that it is all the workers' fault! Those lazy workers would do anything not to work! They probably refused to gather the nectar. But I bet they still wanted all the honey for themselves! Maybe they attacked the Queen to steal it, eh?" she insinuated. "The answer is to make them work harder—no breaks! Limited food rations! That is the way to teach lazy bees and to keep them too bizzy to cause trouble."

"Outrageous!" cried Beeatrice, Queen of Hive Valinstrom. "That doesn't even make sense—if they are lazy by definition, how can they have the drive to overthrow the Queen? The hive is built on the workers. And if they work all the time, when will they have the chance to learn more effective ways of making honey?" she demanded.

"Learn? Learn! They do not need to learn! They only need to work for the Queen! She is the only one who matters! You are too naïve—you do not know how deceptive these workers can be!" retorted Beelzibar.

"I respectfully disagree with her Highness, the Queen of Chernoboch," broke in the Queen of La Ruche République. "It is not the workers but the leaders who must be to blame! The workers give all they have, but the rich, they take it away and leave them with nothing. In my hive, the workers have their rights. We don't produce so much honey, but we are happy!" she concluded.

"I think that we must look for the problem in some sickness that is spreading. It may be some form of germ warfare! We are all at risk!" shouted the Queen of Hive Allerbeste.

"We are all getting so upset! Who can think with all these shouting?! I say we take a break and open a nice bottle of wine. I have a lovely vintage here" soothed the Queen of Il Alveare Rilassato.

At this last suggestion, a fight ensued. Beelzibar spat on the ground at the thought of drinking the proffered wine. Il Alveare's Queen challenged Beelzibar to a duel. The Queen of Allerbeste sided with Alveare against Beelzibar. But before an evil axis could form, Beeatrice and Nectarina separated the members and urged a renewed focus on the problem of hive deaths. The meeting continued long into the night with no resolutions.

As morning dawned, the B-8 summit came to an inconclusive end. All delegates decided to await more information, monitor their hives closely, and maintain sharp contact with each other. Hopefully a clear cause-and-effect pattern would emerge that would allow them to prevent future hive deaths. The Queens flew home exhausted and discouraged.

As she flapped wearily through the air, Beeatrice worried about her hive. Were they happy? Were they next?

CHAPTER TWO

A PICTURE OF HIVE VALINSTROM

"Your Majesty, we have all the cells on the north side filled, and the larvae are progressing nicely," reported Hivey.

Beeatrice stood on the main catwalk overlooking the hive's network of combs. Her North-side unit floor manager, Hivey, gave her the morning report.

"Thank you, Hivey. I'm very pleased with your diligence and progress in the North-side unit. Tell the workers to take an extra half-hour during their designated reading break today," replied Beeatrice, as her court bees conducted her first-hour cleaning.

"Very good, your Majesty. The workers will be so pleased. We have been wanting to read more of the new book you gave us: Formulas for Success: A Queen's Guide to Colony Substances," responded Hivey, and she flew back to the North-side unit.

Beeatrice observed her workers from the catwalk. She watched them going about their various tasks. They performed their duties as expertly as surgeons. The larvae nurse bees fed the royal jelly to their developing brood. The pupae nurses prepared their charges for life outside the cell by feeding them a special diet of pollen and honey. The heater bees maintained the optimum nursery temperature required for a successful growth

environment. Scouts gave their waggle dances to alert foragers to premium nectar sources. And the foragers continually flew to and from the fields, bringing in nectar and pollen then heading back out for more.

She saw Petals carefully cleaning the inside of a cell—she was the most meticulous washer on the North side! And Zinny laying down wax faster than any other bee in the colony! She marveled again at the endless network of combs storing honey for fuel and pollen for nourishment, stores that would allow them to survive the winter.

She was proud of her hive and its productivity. But more than that, Beeatrice believed that everyone truly valued her own work and felt truly valued herself. She would miss those bees left behind after the swarm. She was leaving a few of her best workers to train the developing larvae once they hatched and to serve her successor, the future Queen Buzzi.

Suddenly her face fell. What if these happy bees were the next to disappear? What if Valinstrom collapsed after the swarm? What if her colonies, too, would fall victim to this nameless enemy destroying so many hives? With a heavy heart, she turned from the production floor toward her audience room. She must find a way to prevent tragedy from befalling her workers.

CHAPTER THREE

Beeatrice sat thoughtfully on her throne as Bumble, her herald, read the list of the day's appointments. The morning held one major audience—she always allowed extra time for Buzzi, her protégé. Beeatrice looked forward to her meetings with Buzzi, next in line to take the throne of Valinstrom after the upcoming swarm. Of all her queenly progeny, Buzzi was the most trustworthy bee and the most voracious learner.

Bumble announced Buzzi, who flew brightly into the audience chamber.

"Good morning, Buzzi!" acknowledged Beeatrice.

"Good morning, your Majesty," Buzzi responded. "Thank you for seeing me today."

"What is it you would like us to consider this morning?" asked Beeatrice.

"Your Majesty," began Buzzi, "you have always been most generous with your knowledge and your time. We've spent many hours discussing the swarm plans, the task division in the hive, and the various timetables for production. And yet I do not feel prepared to take over Valinstrom as queen. I'm not sure I understand how to lead these workers. How do you get them to do what you want? How do you make the hive successful?"

Beeatrice considered a moment. Buzzi was asking the right questions—the questions that showed she was ready to lead the hive. It was time for the most important lessons of all.

"Buzzi, your question is a revealing one that tells me the swarm time is near. It's true that I have taught you the logistics of honey production, comb design, nursery maintenance, and hive organization—information that you will now need to apply in a higher-stakes game," began Beeatrice. "But as you suggest, running a hive is more than knowing the details of daily business, though that is also essential. We need to talk about the broader philosophy behind hive governance.

"When thinking about the structure of a bee society, you need to be a student of history. In the past—and even in the present— Queen bees have generally failed to teach their worker bees how to be Queen bees themselves one day if they so choose," Beeatrice continued. "They become greedy and want to keep the honey for themselves. They believe that education encourages workers to be dissatisfied with their positions, thus causing them to produce less honey and hurting the Queen's interests as well as the hive's. They also fear that teaching others to be Queens will threaten their own rule. However, these undesirable outcomes do not have to be the result of education."

"But how can a Queen keep her workers from wanting more for

themselves? Doesn't everyone want to be successful?" inquired Buzzi.

"The Queens are smart," Beeatrice replied. "They find ways to lead the masses where they want them to go. A common technique that Queen bees across the world use to keep their workers prisoners to their jobs is to make them afraid of becoming Queen bees," Beeatrice theorized. "The Queens assure them that they would not be able to pay their bills consistently and that their 'stability'—in other words, a guaranteed stipend of honey—would be gone. Without this stability, they might lose their hives, and their drones would leave them."

"Oh. When you put it that way, I feel a little nervous about leading my own hive," buzzed Buzzi. "I can see why workers stay workers. How will I maintain stability?"

"The first thing to maintaining stability is realizing that this 'stability' is a façade," observed Beeatrice. "A worker can lose her job just as easily as we can lose our hives. Both positions involve risk, and both can fail. If you're going to take a risk, why not take a big one? It's not any more dangerous being a queen than being a worker if you're measuring by stability," concluded Beeatrice.

At that moment, Beeatrice and Buzzi were interrupted by Pollena, the head Scout bee. "Your Majesty," Pollena began, "You said you wanted us to inform you when the flower yields started to change. The scouts are about to meet to discuss their

findings. Would you like to attend the meeting?" she asked.

"Yes, Pollena, and thank you for the notice. I will be there directly," said Beeatrice.

"Thank you, your Majesty. We will await your presence in the Break Room," ended Pollena, who then flew to the Scout Break Room.

"Buzzi, I'm afraid our interview will have to continue later. I will meet you in the training room in two hours," announced Beeatrice.

CHAPTER FOUR

BEELZIBAR

Meanwhile, far away in Hive Chernoboch, Queen Beelzibar had just returned from the B-8 Emergency Summit and was in a foul mood. She ripped through the comb, leaving a trail of stings in her wake. Her court attendants clambered to keep up with her. "Stop cleaning me!" Beelzibar shouted to her Ladies in Waiting. As she flashed past her secretary, she spat, "I do not wish to be disturbed, especially by the rabble!" With that, she slammed the door to her Royal Study. Her faithful attendants collided with the door and fell to the ground in a heap.

Beelzibar stared out the Study's stained glass window to the lush, tropical countryside beyond. "Twenty workers spent a good portion of their lives creating this one window. One of them died from exposure to the chemicals. But I have the most beautiful hive in the southern hemisphere!" she whispered softly to herself. "And I refuse to lose it!"

Beelzibar sat down in her sculpted-wax, honey-encrusted chair. She completed her usual check-list of office security. She had an emergency stash of honey and pollen in her study cabinet as well as her own personal premium supply in the Royal Pantry.

Locked away in her safe were the secret formulas for the honey, the royal jelly for the developing worker larvae, and the royal jelly for herself and the developing queen larvae. She also had wax logistics and comb blueprints under lock and key. Beelzibar was taking no chances that the secrets of a successful hive would get out to her workers.

Over her morning mead, Beelzibar reflected on her rise to power. She had been given her position by biological chance: she had been one of the lucky larvae chosen by the workers to develop into a queen. Then her natural determination had enabled her to leave her cell first and destroy the other queens before they could hatch and challenge her. In the beginning, she had focused on building a strong hive and enhancing the colony—that was the bee way! But as time neared for her to swarm and give up the hive she had worked so hard to create, she began to rethink the "bee way." Why should she give up her home, her study, and her beautiful hive and start over from scratch? The colony existed to serve her—she was the smart one, the strong one. She decided to continue in her role as Supreme Leader and refused to allow any new queens to be born. She knew that some of her managers were lazy and corrupt, but for a small price, they enabled her to maintain absolute control. A few sacrifices were necessary to achieve her goal.

And now this! This pandemic of hive deaths threatened her supremacy from the outside. Since she didn't know the cause, she couldn't guard against it. All her work might still fail. She checked her email and saw that the other B-8 queens were reporting, but none of them had any new information.

Beelzibar next moved to her surveillance screens. She'd installed them recently to allow her to check hive progress and behavior without needing to leave her study. All was proceeding as usual on the various combs. But what was that blur in the corner of the South-west comb? Some strange activity there—she would need to check it out. With a sigh, Beelzibar heaved herself up from her chair and headed to the main production area. It was always something with these workers!

CHAPTER FIVE

LIFE IN HIVE CHERNOBACH

Beelzibar flew down to the production combs. She spoke with her South-west floor manager, who was on her third mead break for the day. "What is the status of honey production on the South-west side?" she demanded.

"We currently run a surplus. As per your instructions, the premium nectar gets funneled to your special storage cells in the Royal Pantry, where the Royal Kitchen bees process it into honey. I have a small batch on reserve in my penthouse comb suite. The workers concentrate the remaining nectar into honey and then cap it for their own use. I make sure they only get one honey break a day! So we always have plenty to 'save,'" she replied with a confidential wink.

"Very good. I thought I saw something strange growing on the edge of the south-west comb. Would you know what that might—" Beelzibar stopped as a clumsy, older bee bumped into her. She turned fierce eyes on the intruder, who cowered under her stare.

"Please, your Majesty. I'm very sorry, I'm sure! I just returned from a 4- kilometer foraging flight—my third one of the day, having had only a mouthful of honey" she squeaked. "I lost control of my wings. Please forgive me, your Majesty" she begged.

"Clumsy oaf!" shrieked Beelzibar. "If you weren't so lazy, rations would be bigger! Go back out and gather more nectar."

"But your Majesty," intervened her right-hand bee, Propolisa, "she's weak as it is. She might not make it back if you send her out again. Let me get a different bee to do it. I'm sure Ms. Jellyby will be more careful next time."

"I'm sure she will because she will learn her lesson this time!" screamed Beelzibar. "I don't need you interceding on behalf of lazy bees! These bees work for me—and I will not allow them to disrupt my organization! They receive more rations than they need anyway," she replied coldly.

As commanded, Ms. Jellyby returned to the fields, struggling with fatigue. Propolisa watched her go with a heavy heart. Ms. Jellyby had been her nurse when she had hatched and had helped Propolisa out of her cell. She worried that her old nurse would not return.

Beelzibar continued her inspection, forgetting the blur on the security screen—a small, thimble-shaped cell hanging half-hidden on the edge of the comb. Instead, she turned her attention to the various floor managers, assessing the honey status across the hive. Then she returned to her study for tea.

Propolisa stayed behind to await Ms. Jellyby's return, but she waited in vain.

CHAPTER SIX

NEW INFORMATION

Back in Valinstrom, Beeatrice flew into her office after a very satisfying report on the nectar sources. She was scheduled to meet Buzzi in half an hour. In the meantime, she planned to have her morning coffee and to check her emails. Her hivekeeper, Ms. Sweeten, brought in the coffee and some delicious honey cakes. She settled herself into her large, waxwork chair and turned on her computer.

Her inbox showed a number of messages from fellow Queens around the world. Ah! Here was an update from Nectarina: "My fellow B-8 leaders, we are getting closer to finding answers on the Hive Death situation. The forensic team recently arrived on the scene of a collapsed colony only moments after the disaster. They found the hive empty except for the queen, the brood nursery, and a few newly-hatched worker bees. Even the honey had been left! The queen was too disoriented to provide helpful information on the collapse, but we are reviving her and hope to get her story soon. We will send details as they become available. Look to your hives!"

"Hmmm," thought Beeatrice. "What strange behavior from bees! To abandon the brood, queen, and honey seems contrary to every bee instinct. What can cause bees to act in such a bizarre way?"

As she puzzled over this new information, another email caught her eye. It was from Beelzibar, and its subject line was alarming: The hive has collapsed.

"What?! Two emails on collapse in one day!" exclaimed Beeatrice.

She opened the message and read quietly to herself: "Queen Beeatrice—you should know that the Enemy has come to Chernoboch! You may be next! All production has stopped. The workers are rioting. I have barricaded myself in my office, but I hear the inevitable sound of coming destruction. It is at my door—the whole hive is shaking. Look to yourselves, but remember me also. The death comes from…"

Here the message ended. Beeatrice sat stunned, staring at the computer screen. What to make of it? Had Beelzibar enjoyed an early cocktail hour? Or had the Enemy come to Chernoboch? This behavior did not seem to fit the pattern of bees abandoning the hive—these bees were overtaking it! But perhaps Beelzibar now knew the answer to the question of what was causing hive deaths.

Beeatrice decided to send an email and wait for a response. If she heard nothing from Beelzibar by nightfall, she would send a team of scouts to Chernoboch. Beeatrice typed, "Are you in trouble? Do you need our help? What is the Enemy? Please respond immediately" and hit "Send."

CHAPTER SEVEN

A SUCCESSFUL LEADERSHIP MODEL

After finishing her coffee, Beeatrice flew to the training room to continue her session with Buzzi. With difficulty, she pushed Beelzibar's email to the back of her mind and tried to focus on the upcoming lessons. She entered the training room and found Buzzi already at a desk, laptop in hand, ready to recommence.

"Ah! I see you are ready to continue the discussion!" said Beeatrice.

"As I remember, we were talking about teaching workers to be their own queens," mused Beeatrice. "You may have noticed that every year I offer a training class for those who wish to be queens and eventually start their own hives. I graduate those students who pass the class. The most recent class ended just before you hatched, and I graduated five bees. I then make sure those graduates do not receive the Queen's substance, which normally suppresses their ovaries. Thus they become fertile. For every bee who graduates, I throw a special wedding, where she, her drones, and a dowry of workers go off to start a new hive. Then she pays me tribute in honey and pollen every year. Thus I propagate the hive through swarming with my successor queens and through franchises with my workers! This process ensures our survival—not our downfall.

"So, a key thing to remember is that helping your workers be successful leaders does not threaten your own leadership but enhances it and helps to ensure your success. Instead of depending on one hive for honey, I have my main hive, plus a 10% broker fee from ten franchise hives, plus resource connections from daughter hives. Even though I work at one hive, my investments look as if I worked at two hives, and that portfolio increases every year!" Beeatrice concluded triumphantly.

"It seems so easy to be successful when I look at you," sighed Buzzi, "but how do I do it? I feel like I don't know the first thing about leading! I get into these discussions on my Facebook page to see what other soon-to-be-queens think, and they all have such different answers! Most of the time they just say, 'The queen gets all the honey! Who cares about the rest?!" said Buzzi, hopelessly.

"Though many bees find themselves in positions to lead, few of them do it well. If you're one of the few who bothers to ask the question, then you'll be one of the few to succeed," encouraged Beeatrice. "Effective leadership remains the key to success in your hive and in every area of life."

Beeatrice continued, "As you know, to get ahead in this world, a bee has to be her own queen. Since you know this fact, you have a duty to teach your workers the same thing and to encourage those who have the drive and the talent to be their own queens. But not everyone wants to be her own queen. No matter how much you show them the beauty of leadership and self sufficiency, some bees will still want to be worker bees. That's okay too."

"What do I do for all those bees—most of the workers—who don't want to be queens? How do I lead them without just taking the honey they make?" inquired Buzzi.

"For those workers, you must show them respect and model diligence and responsibility. Remember Buzzi: just because your bees choose to work for you with no ambition to be queens, they are not slaves. They are your peers. Your equals. Your sisters. Show them love and patience. They will produce for you, and you in turn will create a safe place for them. Never forget what Mother BeeResa said, 'Above all, BEE kind.' Regardless of the bee's ultimate choice, you have a duty to enlighten all your workers and show them the way to success. By encouraging the bees who wish to be queens and by educating and respecting those who stay workers, you create a successful, thriving hive."

"To help new queens prepare for leadership, I created a PowerPoint presentation, which I will show you now," said Beeatrice.

CHAPTER EIGHT

A LESSON ON GENEROSITY

Beeatrice dimmed the lights, booted up her laptop, and turned on the projector. On the screen, Buzzi noted the title, "Six Attributes of a Successful Leader," and typed it in her notes. Beeatrice began her presentation.

"The first lessons pertain to your successful relationship with your workers. They help you create a strong foundation for encouraging the best work from your bees," Beeatrice explained.

Bee mindful of where you come from.

"Buzzi, the hive would never succeed without the bees who work hard day in and day out. Remember that you, too, once performed some of these duties. I make sure all my future queens have 'worker' experience so that they understand a hive's functioning from the ground up. Never be too proud to talk to your subordinates or to help with the 'lower' tasks if the needs arise. Forgetting to take care of those who make the hive possible, or seeing certain jobs as 'beneath' you, will both lead to disaster."

Bee loved, not feared.

"One school of thought preached by Beeavelli suggests that it is better for a ruler to be feared rather than loved because fear is more dependable and better ensures her (usually selfish) goals. But I believe the opposite is true. Love creates a work environment where everyone flourishes and where workers can achieve their maximum potential, thus ensuring the maximum success for the hive. Perhaps the Queen sacrifices the ability to have her every whim fulfilled—for a time—but she achieves greater harmony and stability in the process. A Queen who is willing to go to the end of the world for her bees will find that they will do the same for her. You must KNOW that. Think about your workers as bees, not just producing units."

Bee aware that respect is earned
and not commanded.

"In the same vein, treat all bees with the same respect that you feel you deserve. Earned respect is much more powerful than commanded respect, just as love is more powerful than fear in the long run. You show respect when you listen thoughtfully to a worker's ideas and reward her efforts, when you see her as a bee and remember she has feelings. However, you must be careful not to confuse respect with familiarity: you are the Queen, the hive's leader. The workers look to you as their authority, so always lead by example and hold yourself high with confidence."

"Once you establish this hive culture, then you can cultivate its fruit by wisely leading your workers in hive business," continued Beeatrice.

Bee a Motivator.

"You must get all the bees invested in the hive's progress. Every bee must have her role, but within those assigned tasks, allow for creativity. Be open-minded about the workers' jobs and ideas. If a bee feels she has some ownership of her work and her hive, she will be motivated to help it prosper. You keep your bees motivated by giving them some agency over their projects, listening to their ideas, and being willing to change. Bees in this kind of working environment maintain a sense of pride and feel important to the hive process. Thus they want to help the hive succeed. Remember a happy bee makes more honey."

Bee innovative.

"This goes back to my previous point: Listen to new ideas and always be open to change because some of the most promising innovations may come from workers. Never stop looking for better and more efficient ways to run the hive, produce more honey, and make happier bees. The landscape changes; you must change as well if you are to succeed. For millennia, bees have changed to adapt to their environments—if we stop changing, we die."

Bee an educator

"Above all, you have a duty to educate yourself and your workers. A Queen should never say, "Ok, now I know everything! I don't need to learn any more!" No! Education is a continuous process—you should always be learning. Moreover, you cannot build a hive empire by yourself. You must have help and support from other bees who possess good judgment, a strong knowledge base, and creative ideas. You achieve this kind of bee population by educating your workers. Share your knowledge and give other bees the opportunity to do bigger and better things. Don't try to do everything yourself. Allow your strengths, such as leadership, to flourish and allow other bees to work in their strengths. Also accept help for your weaknesses. In this hive situation, everyone works to the advantage of the hive."

"These key attributes are essential to you developing a successful hive," ended Beeatrice. "I would like to stay and discuss your questions, but at this time, I must see to an urgent situation developing elsewhere in the bee world. Be sure to record your thoughts, and we will continue this discussion later." With this abrupt conclusion, Beeatrice flew quickly out of the room. Buzzi sat quietly for a while and pondered her words.

CHAPTER NINE

The training session over, Beeatrice flew back to her office, anxious to see if any news had arrived from Chernoboch. Disappointingly, she found no new messages in her inbox. The hive-death pandemic remained grave, so Beeatrice decided to act. She sent for the head scout, Pollena, and four of her best comrades. She gave them orders to fly to Chernoboch, assess the situation, and report their findings as soon as possible. After receiving their instructions, the five scouts bowed to the queen and then immediately set out at top speed for Chernoboch.

Upon their arrival, four scout bees took up hidden positions around the hive entrance while Pollena approached the door. Where guard bees should have been posted, she found an empty doorway and empty corridors. She signaled to the others that the entrance was clear and that they should wait for her reconnaissance report. Cautiously, she entered the hive.

Once inside she was aware of a loud and confused clamor of voices and vibrations. The communications were unclear to Pollena. As no one seemed to be guarding the comb, she moved further in to discover the source of the noise. The hive seemed unusually hot, and the wax felt soft beneath her feet as she tiptoed across the first comb. She traveled unnoticed for so long that she decided to risk being discovered and fly her way into the hive's

interior. Here she found the source of the commotion: a large group of worker bees was rioting in front of the Royal Study. Looking up, however, Pollena could see that Beelzibar was imprisoned high above her royal quarters. She crept inside an empty cell to eavesdrop on the protest.

"Propolisa! You and your new Queen get out here!" shouted an aggressive-looking bee leading the crowd. "We won't stay here forever! We're not indentured servants! We are bees, just like you. If you can't set things right, we'll swarm on our own and find a new hive," she threatened.

The office door opened. Propolisa came out to the crowd. "Dahly… workers… we ask for your patience," soothed Propolisa. "None of you thought a coup would happen easily, did you? We just need more time to organize a new government—" but Dahly interrupted her.

"More time? The hive is in chaos as it is! We cannot forage and bring in more honey because the wax isn't conducting our signals as usual! The larvae are dying in their cells for reasons we don't understand. Most of us are starving and won't have the strength to forage once you do 'organize.' How is it that you don't know what you are doing? If one more thing goes wrong, the colony will be doomed!" screeched Dahly.

Pollena had heard enough. She crept out of her cell and back outside to her scouts. Upon arrival, she apprised them of the situation and quickly texted Beeatrice: "Hive in trouble. Sending Stripey back w/ full report. More l8r. P"

CHAPTER TEN

A TELLING CONCLUSION

Stripey arrived early the next morning to fill Beeatrice in on the situation. "Thank you for your diligence, Stripey. You've given me a lot of information. I know you have flown a tremendous distance in the past twenty-four hours. Get some rest and recuperate while I decide what to do," she said.

"Thank you, your Majesty," replied Stripey, who bowed and flew wearily out of Beeatrice's study.

Beeatrice began putting the pieces together. A new Queen. A revolt. A malfunctioning hive. A riot. A threat to swarm.

What if the Enemy wasn't external? What if it originated in the hive itself?

Beeatrice sketched a possible timeline of colony collapse:

1) A new queen emerges without the approval of the reigning queen. [(Why?) she wrote in parenthesis and underlined twice.]

2) The new queen and her supporters take over the hive without appropriate swarm preparation. (Again, why?)

3) Something goes wrong in the hive, and the new regime

quickly gets into trouble. (What could go so wrong?)

4) Perhaps a catastrophe occurs, forcing the colony to abandon the hive.

5) The bees swarm. But what happens to the new hive? It doesn't seem that the resulting hive establishes itself enough to remain a viable colony because we never find it.

Beeatrice continued to wonder: What could cause bees—normally such coordinated and cooperative beings—to revolt? And how could the new leadership fail so quickly?

Beeatrice needed answers to these questions and felt she should visit the scene herself. The rest of the bee world and perhaps Valinstrom—soon to be Buzzi's hive—were at stake. In any case, it sounded like many lives were at stake in Chernoboch itself.

Beeatrice texted Pollena her plan: "I want to visit. Can u arrange it? B."

CHAPTER ELEVEN

A FAILED COUP

Back in Chernoboch, Pollena had decided to make a formal visit to Propolisa. Propolisa had managed to appease the crowd—for the moment. Pollena knew her time was short to intervene. She had only a few minutes to speak with Propolisa before the workers took matters into their own hands.

She flew back into the hive. Again, no guard bees were on duty and none of the listless workers seemed to notice a strange bee in their hive. Pollena flew to the Royal Office Suite. A secretary had timidly returned to her post after the rioters dispersed. She looked startled at the appearance of a foreigner in the Royal Office area.

"Quick," whispered Pollena. "We don't have much time! The workers will not remain satisfied for long. Get me in to see Propolisa! I am Pollena, lead scout from Hive Valinstrom. I'm here on orders from her highness Queen Beeatrice. She sent me to investigate the disruption of your hive."

The secretary nodded and flew quickly to the Study door. She opened it abruptly and announced, "An emissary from Hive Valinstrom here to see you on orders from Queen Beeatrice, ma'am," and moved aside for Pollena to enter.

"What the—" began Propolisa indignantly, but Pollena cut her off.

"You're in trouble. Anyone can see that this hive is doomed. If you don't act fast, you'll lose the hive and the workers will lose their lives. Is that what you want?" demanded Pollena.

"Of course not! But what can I do? Nothing we try works! When the wax is too soft, everything fails. We can't seem to communicate effectively with each other. The brood is failing to thrive. We're doing tings the way we've always done—or so we thought—but it's not working!" wailed Propolisa.

"You've got to ask for help. I have three other scouts with me— we can at least start trouble-shooting. Have you even thought to ask Beelzibar what's going on?" inquired Pollena.

"She only sits in her cell and sulks! But I see her smirking behind her attempts to look pathetic and puzzled," said a frustrated Propolisa.

"We have to bring in someone who knows—hold on. I'm getting a text message." Pollena reached for her cell phone and read Beeatrice's message. She smiled triumphantly as she turned to Propolisa. "Queen Beeatrice has requested an audience. She would like to visit the hive to offer her assistance in maintaining the colony."

Propolisa smiled for the first time all day. "Yes! Have her Majesty come, and I will see her!"

Pollena texted her response: "ur n."

CHAPTER TWELVE

BEATRICE'S INTERVENTION

The fact that Queen Beeatrice was on her way bought Propolisa more time with her disgruntled workers. They agreed to stay until the queen arrived, but they continued to buzz listlessly around the combs. No one foraged. The nurse bees fed the brood, but little more. Pollena and her scouts had left to meet Queen Beeatrice mid-flight and escort her the rest of the way to Chernoboch.

As Propolisa sat in Beelzibar's study absorbing a few moments of quiet in an otherwise raucous day, the hive's malaise was suddenly broken by a tumultuous commotion. The hive rocked, and for the first time since the riot, the bees stirred themselves into action. An invader! A mouse had penetrated the hive bent on finding the honey and larvae. The bees marshaled into attack formation, stinging the mouse repeatedly as it struggled to crawl across the combs. But the mouse was no match for a squadron of angry bees: it soon collapsed from the wounds and died on the hive floor. Those bees whose stings found their mark died alongside their victim.

When the bees had neutralized the threat, they stood back, exhausted by their exertion. They were already weakened by the lack of honey and pollen, and this final push had further depleted their reserves. Some of the bystander bees mournfully

swept the dead bee carcasses out of the hive as the remaining bee population saluted their fallen comrades.

Now, however, Propolisa's bees had a bigger problem—what to do with the mouse carcass? Mice are full of disease and parasites. It would be only a matter of time before its decomposing body contaminated their home. But it was too big to move! Panic set in with bees buzzing wildly about the comb, wondering how to contain the new and graver threat of colony-wide infection and destruction. No one seemed to know what to do, the new queen least of all.

The bees closest to the carcass began to wobble and weaken. They hit the wax with a thud. More distant ranks moved in to sweep them out, thus removing the contagion, but to little effect as the mouse carcass remained.

No solution presented itself to the workers.

Just when the bees had given up the hope of fixing the problem and were preparing for a sudden and doomed swarm, Pollena buzzed in to announce Queen Beeatrice's arrival. She stopped mid-sentence when she saw the mouse carcass. Beeatrice followed quickly on her wings and began rapidly giving orders: "Find your store of propolis quickly! Take my scouts with you—they know this drill."

"Propolis? We don't know where Beelzibar keeps it!" shrieked Propolisa.

"Pollena, take me to the royal secretary" Beeatrice commanded. "Propolisa clearly has not been given the necessary information to lead this hive. And at this point, she's too panicked to think clearly," Beeatrice wryly observed as she watched Propolisa zoom head-first into an empty cell and stay there.

Pollena quickly led Beeatrice to the Royal Office Suite. The secretary remained at her post, though frightened. "Listen to me," ordered Beeatrice calmly, "I need to know where Queen Beelzibar keeps her private reserve honey and jelly and such."

"I don't know!" wailed the secretary. "She would never tell anyone!"

Beeatrice realized that none of the bees had been given the information necessary to conduct hive affairs in Beelzibar's absence. The corrupt floor managers had her cell phone number, so she always communicated with them when she traveled from home. They, of course, fled when they realized the coup had succeeded. Beelzibar must have believed this system of fractured and compartmentalized information would ensure worker dependence on the queen, and thus the queen's absolute control of the hive!

She had Pollena lead her to Beelzibar's cell. Beelzibar sat crumpled and forlorn against a wall, unaware of the catastrophe brewing below. "Beelzibar! We need the location of the propolis stores," demanded Beeatrice. "Tell me where they are."

"Beeatrice! What are you doing here? Have you come to save me?" pleaded Beelzibar.

"I've come to save your hive. If we don't save it, you won't be around for us to save! A mouse has blundered into the hive and been killed, but your bees don't know how to neutralize the infection threat. You'll die a very unpleasant death soon if you don't tell me where those stores are! And I will leave you here to rot if you refuse to help your own workers!" snapped Beeatrice.

Beelzibar's face twisted into a sour expression, but she realized Beeatrice would not bargain with her. Reluctantly, she parted with the information: "Look under the floor board below the desk in my study" she pouted.

Beeatrice whisked out of the jail and flew down to the study to retrieve the propolis. She and Pollena took it to the bees trying to contain the mouse carcass. "Spread this over the mouse," Beeatrice commanded, "as quickly as you can. Don't mind if you get some on yourselves either—it will do you good."

Within a matter of seconds, the bees had contained the threat. The mouse was mummified. The last dead worker had been pushed out of the hive, and everyone breathed a sigh of relief. The colony had been saved!

CHAPTER THIRTEEN

A GENEROUS RESTORATION

After saving the hive from certain calamity, Beeatrice and Propolisa next had to find food and fuel for the remaining bees. Luckily, one floor manager, Beedora, had stayed behind after the coup. She had been asleep and so hadn't managed to escape before the new regime came to power. Since the coup, she had been hiding in her penthouse comb suite reserved for Chernoboch Bee elite. Beeatrice and Propolisa found her in their search for food, and she lead them to the private honey stores that she and the other managers kept.

With these supplies, Beeatrice and Propolisa were able to save the colony from starvation. They strategically doled them out to the remaining workers such that the mature, foraging bees had enough fuel to bring in more nectar. They also ensured that the nurse bees and heater bees had sufficient nutrition and fuel to care for the brood. The receiver bees got the smallest rations as they would remain on the comb, calmly waiting to accept the nectar brought by the foragers. Their main share would be the less-caloric but still satisfying nectar brought by the foragers until the honey stores were back to full capacity.

After feeding the bees, Beeatrice next turned her attention to the nursery. She assembled the brood heater bees first. Pointing to the thermometer on the wall, she said, "This thermometer

registers the brood temperature for this nursery. It should remain at 35°C. You can use your antenna to sense if you get a few degrees above or below this target. That range is permissible, though it will result in workers that vary slightly in their sensitivity to stimuli." Beeatrice turned to the Charge Nurse. "Charge Nurse, I leave you here to monitor the brood thermometer and regulate the 'filling station' bees who will keep the heaters energized for their work," she instructed.

"Yes, your Majesty. Thank you, your Majesty! I was so worrit about me larvae!" she sobbed gratefully.

Finally, Beeatrice turned her attention to the biggest job: she had to get the comb back in shape. How could foragers or anyone else communicate if the comb wasn't conducting signals as usual? She assembled the receiver bees waiting on their cells for the returning foragers. "Your charge today as you await the return of the foragers is to repair the comb and to cool the hive so the wax conducts signals successfully," she explained. Pointing to a cluster of bees standing on the shattered comb, she commanded, "First, I want you lot to repair the crumbled cells destroyed by the mouse and the heat. If you find you need more fuel or food to complete your job, alert the new floor manager, and she will contact me," said Beeatrice.

"Second, the rest of you need to begin cooling the hive. Use as little energy as possible, but if you all hang from the lowest cells and vibrate your wings gently, you should be able to form an air current that will cycle the hot air out of the comb and generate cooler air to harden the wax" she directed. "We want that thermometer reading 32°C! You with the book—you're the new floor manager. You're in charge."

"Yes, your Majesty. With pleasure, your Majesty!" she replied.

Within minutes, Beeatrice's tactics had restored order and stability to the hive. The workers laying the wax had reconstructed the shattered comb, providing new cells for pollen and honey. The heater and cooler bees had adjusted the temperature to facilitate the brood growth in the nursery as well as the communication signals from returning scouts and foragers. The receiver bees busily accepted the pollen and nectar from the incoming foragers, storing the pollen and capping the honey cells.

After handling the comb needs, Beeatrice returned to the nursery to instruct the nurse bees on preparing the royal jelly. "How is it that you ladies don't know the way to mix the larval formula? Taking care of the brood is your job!" she exclaimed.

"We know, your Majesty, but Beelzibar kept all that information to herself, di'n she? She had everythin' pre-measured and jus' said, 'Add this to this.' And we always had the managers tellin' us what to do. Now that our stores are depleted, we don' know how to make it from scratch, and the Queen and managers are gone!

I think Propolisa knew, but she di'n see fit to share it either," Nurse Joy humbly replied.

"That's ridiculous! Ignorance only creates weak bees! I'm putting the recipe up here on the wall so that you will know how to make it yourselves and can be responsible for your work. The important part is that you only want a 10% hexos solution for worker bees! And once they reach pupa stage, discontinue the royal jelly for the workers—feed them honey and pollen" she commanded.

CHAPTER FOURTEEN

PROPOLISA'S EXPLANATION

By the day's end, the hive had been restored to normal. The receiver bees had signaled to the foragers that the combs were full, and the troops returned for the night. The nursery was back on track. The comb was in pristine shape. The hive buzzed busily with satisfied and diligent bees.

Beeatrice wearily sat down in a cushy drawing room chair to await the Royal Tea. Propolisa entered timidly and took a chair across from her.

"Propolisa, what happened? How could you take over a hive if you knew nothing about running it?" demanded Beeatrice.

Propolisa sighed. "Well, I didn't realize I didn't know enough. I was Beelzibar's right-hand bee, and I assumed I knew everything she knew. I certainly knew enough to hatch a new queen! But that's where my expertise ended," she explained. Propolisa looked defeated.

"But why did you want to overthrow Beelzibar? What drove you to it?" asked Beeatrice incredulously.

"She had turned into a monster!" Propolisa exclaimed. "She managed to get rid of most of the experienced workers because they might have challenged her. And she trained the new larvae

in a new system of subservience. She gave them partial information and required them to work only one task so that they never learned how the entire colony worked. Then she set up greedy, corrupt managers who ensured the bees never learned but remained reliant on the Queen and her underlings. The managers benefited from this system and so were happy to continue it. They didn't care about the workers!

Propolisa continued, "She took control of every aspect of the hive, confiscated the honey for herself, and showed no interest in the well-being of her workers. Beelzibar was willing to sacrifice her bees to enrich herself. I just got tired of seeing half-starved, hard-working bees living in hovels to satisfy her appetites for power and wealth!

"As her right-hand bee, I saw everything" Propolisa reflected. "It made me sick, and I couldn't support the system any more. I wanted to do something about it. So I convinced a few of my workers to help me hatch a new queen who would replace Beelzibar. But of course, she didn't know how to do anything either. I was truly in charge, though I didn't know how to teach anyone else bee logistics. Then all the managers who at least had some training and knowledge fled out of fear for their lives and property—and well they should, I suppose! So you see what a mess I made of it. But my intentions were good. I didn't think I would need another queen in charge," Propolisa concluded sadly.

Beeatrice looked at Propolisa in sympathy. She helped her to her feet as the hive bell called them in to tea.

CHAPTER FIFTEEN

BEELZIBAR UNREPENTANT

The next day, Beeatrice prepared to leave Chernoboch and return to Valinstrom. She left Propolisa and Queen Marigold in charge of a well-regulated hive. Beeatrice provided copies of the various formulas as well as the hive's logistical instructions in the Royal Library, Propolisa's office, and the comb break rooms. Order had been restored in Chernoboch, and the workers had given the hive a new name: Beegri-la.

Beeatrice was needed at Valinstrom for the appointed swarm. But before leaving, she wanted to talk with Beelzibar. After receiving permission from Propolisa to visit the prisoner, she made her way to Beelzibar's cell.

The prisoner was in a slightly better humor after being well fed, but she still behaved sulkily and warily. Beeatrice sat down on a bench outside of her cell.

"Well? Are you going to just sit there and watch me suffer? Or will you do something to help a fellow queen? We are sisters, you and I. Help me regain my throne!" Beelzibar cajoled.

"It sounds like you made your workers suffer quite a bit. Your situation looks rather comfortable to me," replied Beeatrice coolly.

"You can sit there smugly, but you could be next! We queens must stick together!" she warned.

"No, I don't think my hive will be next. You and I—we have very different systems," Beeatrice countered.

"If you help me regain my throne, I will send you some of my best drones, eh? And some prize honey every month! Think of it—you could get rich quickly," Beelzibar wheedled.

"Do you think I can be bought?! How could you do this to them? They are your workers—your bees from your eggs. You see them every day, bringing you food, enhancing your business. And yet you treat them as sub-bees and withhold from them the knowledge they need to live full and successful lives. How can you live with yourself?" Beeatrice demanded angrily.

"What do you know about it, eh? Do you ever look around you and think, 'I made this hive! I deserve it! It's mine!' Those stupid workers—if they are so smart, so valuable, then how can they allow me to rule them so? Eh? No. I am a Queen. I am one in a million—they are all the same, like ants: interchangeable! Why should I care if they are sad or educated? An educated worker is a threat—she can disagree, she can make new plans to challenge me. An ignorant worker must always play by my rules" Beelzibar triumphantly hissed.

"I was born into this position. I am genetically pre-disposed for greatness. I control the information. I control the security of my hive. I control the honey production. I am the one who takes ALL the risks. I am the ultimate law. I am the most important bee in this hive! Therefore I am the only one who gets ALL the spoils. Period!" she finished triumphantly.

Beeatrice looked at her in disgust. "Look at you now. Just look at yourself!" she challenged. "Do you think you would be a prisoner in your own hive, overthrown by your own children, and defeated by people completely dependent on you if your way were successful? If you were as inherently superior as you claim? Or if your subjects were happy? The answer is NO!

"The formula to riches in leadership is soooo simple," Beeatrice continued. "Take care of the least of your workers, and you will be taken care of tenfold. What queens like you don't understand is that there isn't only one hive that must be divided among all. Rather an infinite number of hives exist to be made and had, an infinite amount of honey to be created. You don't have to rob Beetar to pay Pollena. You can create a happy environment for your family of workers. The result will be not incompetence but generous loyalty. Your workers will do anything for you because at the heart of your system are love and respect. Greed only creates resentment and corruption. Love creates loyalty. Dale CarneBee said it best, 'If you want to gather honey, then don't kick over the beehive.'"

Beelzibar glared at Beeatrice with disdain and pity. "I suppose you really believe that!" she spat. "More's the pity for you! We'll see who has the last laugh. I will rule again! Then I will teach those bees a lesson."

Beeatrice left the interview with a sense of failure. She had not managed to influence Beelzibar's viewpoint at all. She felt sure Beelzibar was unrepentant and would, indeed, plan to retaliate against her own bees, especially if she were ever returned to power. Beeatrice left Hive Beegri-la for Valinstrom with a heavy heart. Though she felt happy to have served the cause of bees everywhere, she felt discouraged by Beelzibar's refusal to change.

CHAPTER SIXTEEN

RETURN TO THE B-8

At the next meeting of the B-8, Beeatrice was the guest speaker. The current Queen of Hive Valincore, she also had ten franchise hives in her region, and Valinstrom continued to thrive. Beeatrice studied her audience as she took the podium to report on the hive death pandemic.

"My fellow queens," she began. "We have all been concerned about the pandemic of hive deaths. We have all wondered whether this new Enemy would reach our combs. My recent experiences with a collapsing hive have shown me that collapse is not inevitable. Each Queen controls the viability of her hive and has the power to stave off destruction.

"The Enemy is not an external one," she continued. "It is an internal enemy bred from ignorance, selfishness, oppression, and a failure to understand bee nature. Bees remain social creatures who must look to each other's interests and the hive's interests to ensure their own survival. When a Queen forgets that she is part of this superorganism and attempts to act on her own selfish interests, she initiates the destruction sequence. When she keeps her bees in ignorance of successful living strategies, she cultivates her own downfall.

"Beelzibar learned this lesson the hard way. Her bees became

tired of serving her interests at the expense of their own, tired of supporting corrupt managers who cared nothing for them. Their impoverished conditions made them susceptible to an alternative leadership plan, but that plan proved to be equally misinformed. Had it not been for my timely intervention, this hive, too, would have failed. Beelzibar lost everything in order to keep a stranglehold on ONE hive at the expense of her workers.

"In contrast, my hive has successfully swarmed, and I have another ten hives that pay me yearly brokerage fees. That number increases every year. I opt for a more open, generous, and egalitarian system. As a consequence, I don't need to focus all my energy on controlling one hive—I focus my energy on creating new hives that operate under their own management and provide me with grateful and fair returns. This system is a win-win for everyone," she proclaimed.

"The newly renamed Hive Beegri-la thrives under a new leader, who will be reinstated to the B-8 at our next annual summit," Beeatrice announced to much applause. "In the meantime, Beelzibar remains under house arrest. Her conditions are satisfactory, though she has been relieved of her position. I do not recommend reinstating her. The bees have chosen a new queen—they have initiated and voted in their entirety on this outcome. We must respect their wishes. After talking with Beelzibar, I do not find her to be repentant. Her actions would enslave her people once again and reset the hive's course on the same destructive path. I recommend that she continues to be restricted by the Beegri-la leadership. And I recommend, too, that every bee here reconsiders her hive and her educational approach when evaluating the hive death threat," concluded Beeatrice, and she sat down.

The B-8 Summit room was once again filled with excited buzzing, but this time that buzzing was relieved and congratulatory. The B-8 representatives wanted to know more about Beeatrice's methods.

"How is this achieved?" demanded the Queen of La Ruche Republique.

"I think we would like to know more about this plan," stated the Queen of Allerbeste.

The demand for Beeatrice's experiences and business approach was so high that Nectarina had to quiet the room and promise that Beeatrice would be available for questions at the session's end. Over the coming weeks, Beeatrice found herself scheduling appointments with hives from the B-8 summit countries and beyond, educating others in developing the most successful, innovative hives with the happiest bees possible.

Only one bee did not rejoice at Beeatrice's success: Beelzibar kept to her cell and complained vociferously to anyone who would listen about her ill treatment at Beeatrice's hand. Under her breath, however, she voiced more threatening opinions.

Buzzi was overjoyed at her mentor's success. She broadcasted Beeatrice's speech from her Facebook page and implemented her lessons to the best of her ability. "She's amazing!" she told her protégé. "I hope I'm like her some day."

And Valincore continued to thrive as Beeatrice directed its affairs, a model for the values of love, respect, and humility at the heart of enterprise.

EPILOGUE

A huddled figure quietly hurried up the narrow, winding stone steps to the top of the palace. Beelzibar's quarters sat high above the colony, remote but comfortable. Though she remained under house arrest, she was not strictly watched twenty-four hours a day. Propolisa did not see her as a threat to the new leadership—none of the workers wanted her back.

The huddled figure had no problem entering the locked apartment. Once inside, she threw off her cloak and announced her presence, "Beelzibar! It's me—Beedora! I have something to show you."

Beelzibar strode haughtily to where Beedora stood in the next room. Beedora had maintained her loyalty to Beelzibar, whom she hoped would one day return to the throne. She missed the days of free honey, a penthouse comb, and endless spa trips. She appeared a reformed bee under the new leadership in order to save her striped skin! But secretly she hoped for a return to the previous administration.

As Beelzibar approached, Beedora opened up her laptop. "I thought you might want to see your friend Beeatrice's speech to de B-8," she began. "Buzzi, her protégé, has posted it to her Facebook page."

Beelzibar watched in mute disgust at Beeatrice's speech. By the end, her face had twisted itself into a nasty smirk: half furious, half malevolent.

"So, she intends to keep me a prisoner here! We'll see about that, Queen Beeatrice…yes, we'll see," she hissed.

ABOUT THE AUTHOR

 Zagros Bigvand was born in Kermanshah, Iran, a son of Kurdish-Iranian parents. He and his family fled Iran after the 1979 Iranian Revolution, and he was raised in Dallas, TX. Zagros' childhood was financially difficult so his ambition from an early age was to become financially independent. By the age of 28 he was a millionaire. Today he has several successful businesses and he supports charities through the proceeds of his business transactions. Zagros loves teaching others how to become financially independent. He has created successful businesses in finance, real estate, construction, and other industries. Zagros believes the reason financial education is so lacking is because the school system is not geared around teaching financial freedom. He has said, "Although their hearts are in the right place, school teachers cannot teach their students to be financially independent unless they, themselves, are financially independent." He believes the best chance at learning to be financially free is to learn from another who is financially free.

Because of the hardships he faced in childhood, Zagros seeks to support others growing up in financial difficulties. He participates in several charitable organizations and seeks to help others through education and charitable giving. This interest in enabling others to be more financially successful, coupled with a personal background involving political revolution inspired him to write his first book, Mind Your Beeswax.

With this book, Zagros conveys to both the Haves and Have-Nots the importance of increasing the public's financial knowledge and success. This expansion of financial knowledge and wealth helps ground a nation's stability and ensure its future success. More importantly, however, generosity—intellectual, financial, and personal—remains central to successful societies, businesses, families, relationships, and a meaningful life.

Find out more about Zagros at http://www.zagrosbigvand.com/